@thespeedofJake

by

Jennifer Maisel

NoPassport Press

@thespeedofJake by Jennifer Maisel

Contact Susan Schulman, A Literary Agency,
for performance rights
susan@schulmanagency.com

NoPassport Press
PO Box 1786
South Gate, CA90280 USA.
Nopassport.org

ISBN: 978-1-4583-4854-8

Jennifer Maisel's *The Last Seder* premiered Off-Broadway with Gaby Hoffmann and Greg Mullavey after productions around the country and abroad. Before its critically acclaimed world premiere at Antaeus theatre in the fall of 2019, Jennifer developed *Eight Nights* with the Berkshire Playwrights Lab, Bay Street Theatre, Playmakers, Moving Arts and Antaeus; that production was nominated for nine coveted Ovation Awards and won for Best Playwriting. The play was also part of nationwide fundraiser for HIAS called 8 nights of EIGHT NIGHTS. Her *Out of Orbit* was workshopped at the Gulf Shore New Play Festival as well as the Sundance Theatre Lab, and was awarded an Ensemble Studio Theatre/Alfred P Sloan rewrite commission for plays about science and technology before making the 2016 Kilroy List and winning both the Stanley Award and the Woodward Newman Award for Drama. It premiered at Williamston Theatre and Bloomington Playwrights Project in 2018. Her Pen West Literary finalist *There or Here* had its London premiere in January, 2018. Her *@thespeedofJake,* also a Pen West Literary finalist, premiered in LA with Playwrights' Arena. Jennifer was one of seven playwrights commissioned by Center Theatre Group and Playwrights' Arena to create *The Hotel Play*, a site-specific work created in commemoration of the 25th anniversary of the LA riots. Jennifer was one of five writers in the prestigious Humanitas 2018 PlayLA workshop, where she wrote her play Better. In April 2021 she was the Travis Bogard Artist in Residence with a Tao House fellowship, writing a new play called Yellow Wallpaper 2.0 2020 on Eugene O'Neill's former estate. A graduate of Cornell University with an MFA from NYU's Tisch School of the Arts' Dramatic Writing Program, Jennifer also writes for film and television. www.jennifermaisel.com

@thespeedofJake premiered in Los Angeles at Playwrights' Arena in November of 2015, artistic director Jon Lawrence Rivera.

The cast and artistic team were as follows

Director – Jon Lawrence Rivera

CLARK – Ryun Yu

EMILY – Elizabeth Pan

SAMANTHA – Celeste Den

RICHARD – David Carey Foster

RENEE - Renee Threatte

Scenic Designer – John Iacovelli
Lighting Designer – Justin Huen
Projection Designer – Tom Ontiveros
Costume Designer – Mylette Nora
Sound Designer/Original Music – Howard Ho
Live Cello – Kate Lee
Casting Director – Raul Staggs
Stage Manager – Veronica Vasquez
Producer – JoAnn Paolantonio
Graphic Designer – Celina T. Duffy

@thespeedofJake

At that edge of Harlem people optimistically call the Upper West Side, it is an apartment inflicted by murkiness.

We don't see people entering at the top of a scene and exiting to end it – they are here, suddenly, as if we woke up to find them standing over us in a room that is suddenly not a dream. They come and they are gone.

The furniture in this place has lost its former status. Computers, clothes, papers, take-out containers flood the dining table; chairs have morphed into trash-piled objects d'crap; the bookshelves that line the walls have become repositories for the growing detritus of daily living. Nothing has left here in a long time.

It is not the apartment of a hoarder, it is the apartment of someone desperately trying to hold on. There is a difference.

I don't know if we ever know what time it is.

CHARACTERS:

CLARK – 40ish, male

EMILY – 40ish, female

SAMANTHA – SAM - Clark's sister

RICHARD – 45, male

RENEE - mid-thirties, female

This play takes place in the not too distant future. These are 21st century friends, families and relationships. When casting, please bear in mind that there are no specifications as to race or ethnicity.

…….. – denotes a response without words

BEFORE

THE EDGE OF THE SOCCER FIELD. THE EDGE OF THE WORLD

Clark and Emily.
Too early Saturday morning clothes.
They have come prepared.
Snacks. Travel coffee mugs.
Two of those camping chairs with sunshades. The kind of things they would have been embarrassed to own a decade ago.
They stand at the line, scanning the field, shading their eyes from the glare of the sun.
Their bodies tell us where Jake is, where he's going next, how fast he is -

EMILY:	CLARK:
Where is he?	I don't see him.

EMILY: There –

CLARK: How the hell does he do that?

EMILY: Teleportation.

CLARK: I'm not fast.
You're not fast.
Not in that way –

(she gives him a look)

EMILY: You wish.

CLARK: I do, I do wish…

EMILY: Rub it three times, baby.

CLARK: Excuse me, I'm watching my kid.

EMILY: *(not yelling)*
Oh my god – defense defense defense! That kid is offsides. Hello? Ref?

CLARK: ….

EMILY: What?

CLARK: You. Sports.
Sports lingo.

EMILY: …..

CLARK: …..

EMILY: Well. Parenting.

CLARK: …

EMILY: What did you get for snack?

CLARK: Chips and chocolate.

EMILY: Clark.

CLARK: And oranges.

EMILY: .....

CLARK: When it comes down to the kids hating me, or the parents, you know I'm always happy to tell the healthy-snack-only brigade to fuck off.

EMILY: Yeah, but it's me they'll email.
It's always – who's the snack mom?

CLARK: Just tell them you can't be 10 more than once –

EMILY: .....
There he goes –

CLARK: There he goes there he goes there he goes ---

EMILY and CLARK: ……

(they edge just a little bit closer to each other)

EMILY and CLARK: ……

(he's working his way down the field)

EMILY and CLARK:
Comeoncomeoncomeoncomeon –

(collectively held breath)

EMILY and CLARK: ……
……..
………..

(GOAL)

ONE

THE APARTMENT

You wouldn't know what time it is in here. Day. Night. It's all the same.

Clark has fallen asleep over the dining room table that functions as his desk, the laptop glows softly beside him, his head pillowed on a mound of papers.

The feel of Jake in the room. The rustle the papers make as he runs by. His footsteps. The wisp of his laughter. He is there and not there.

Clark bolts awake.

He is alone.

TWO

THE APARTMENT

Samantha, Clark

SAM: Where the fuck were you?

(Clark gestures to his surrounds.)

We said we were meeting at the field.

CLARK: We did not.

SAM: Clark –

CLARK: There was no agreement on my part.

SAM: You said you wanted to see the girls –

CLARK: And I do -

SAM: I am not bringing them here.

CLARK: So it's a little messy.

SAM: It's sad, Clark. It's like walking into a pit of grief.

CLARK: Yeah, take them to Disneyland

SAM: Cut it out.

CLARK: Nope –it's clean there. I get it. They got folks whose job it is to make sure the place sparkles.

SAM: They shouldn't have fun. They shouldn't enjoy themselves any more.

CLARK: It's OK for kids to understand what it's like to be sad.

SAM: They do!
If you think they don't miss him – they miss him.

CLARK: Do they talk about him?

SAM: They do –

CLARK: But not as much any more.

SAM: No.

CLARK: Not as much.

SAM: No.

CLARK: How much?

SAM: Clark.

CLARK: How often?

Have they gone from every second to every minute? From every minute to every hour? From once in the morning and once before bed? From once a day to once in a while? From every so often to once in a blue moon?

SAM: They're kids. They don't always say what they feel. Fucking adults don't say what they feel most of the goddamn time, if we even know what we fucking feel.

CLARK: You curse like that in front of the girls.

SAM: Fuck no.

CLARK: That's how I know to you he's gone.

SAM: .....

CLARK: .....

SAM: ....
He is gone, Clark. Not just to me. And for the girls it's been a huge part of their lives that he was here and almost as huge a part that he's not. For Bea – the balance has tipped. More gone than here.

CLARK: Gone, like gone gone gone.

SAM: First step – Denial. First step. First.

CLARK: Fuck denial.
And fuck you.
Since when are you all about that –

SAM: Since for a while.

CLARK: Oh come on –

SAM: Since Jake.

CLARK: Bullshit.

SAM: You like to think that this is all yours, you know that. Well, grief isn't all yours and Jake wasn't only yours.

CLARK: He is now.

SAM: I was sad. I was sad for me and sad for him and sad for the girls and Emily and for you. I was heartbroken for you. And I couldn't move out of it.

CLARK: But you did. You did move out of it.

SAM: I'm just not in it as much.
I'm just not drowning any more. I'm treading.
I can see the shore. I'm hoping I'll get there.
And I'm hoping you'll get there too.

CLARK: What the fuck would I do with myself if I did?

SAM: .....

CLARK: ....

SAM: You have two nieces who miss you and maybe it's an asshole thing for me to want their uncle to be part of their lives but that's what I want and I know I'm not supposed to push you and that at some point you'll come around but you haven't come around and you haven't come around and you're missing so much.

SAM (Cont.): I'm afraid you're going to drown. Fully and completely.

CLARK: Sounds delightful.

SAM: ….

CLARK: ….

SAM: ….

CLARK: *(trying)*
How are the girls?

SAM: You really don't deserve to know.

CLARK: ….

SAM: Lily has a crush. On a boy. A real boy, not a TV boy.

CLARK: She tells you this.

SAM: He has no idea she exists so she kind of dances around him. It's wonderful and horrifying at the same time.

Bea wants to read to me all the time, but, you know, she's 6, she can't read, so it's -

CLARK: The c-c-c-aaaaa--t w-w-w-w-w-weeeeent –

SAM: t-t-t-t-oe, toooooooo th th th the – ac ac ac ac – accccqua -

CLARK: There should be a moratorium on kids' books that have animals doing things against their feral nature. What cat goes to an aquarium without wanting to Roman binge on the fish instead of studying them?

SAM: Fucking over-civilized cat.

CLARK: Doing kids a huge disservice making them read to us about giddy animals -

SAM: - brainwashing them into thinking animals' true nature is to be nice to each other. I mean, did we read to Mom and Dad? Did they read to us?

CLARK: They must have –

SAM: But we don't remember that, right? Which is what I was thinking last night when it took her so long to sound out an eight word sentence that I forgot the beginning before she got to the end – who's going to remember this?

CLARK: ….

SAM: ….

CLARK: ….

SAM: I know.

CLARK: You don't know –

SAM: OK, I don't know. I know a little. Just a little.

CLARK: …..

SAM: …..

CLARK: …..

SAM: ….

THREE

THE APARTMENT

Emily, Clark

EMILY: Hello.

CLARK: What are you doing here?

EMILY: Yeah, um, most people say hello.

CLARK: Most people knock.

EMILY: ….

CLARK: We're past that - hello. We're way the hell past goodbye.

EMILY: I knocked.

CLARK: You didn't knock.

EMILY: Prove it. And you have some drool right there.

CLARK: What are you doing here?
And why do you still have a key?

EMILY: It's still half mine.

CLARK: What are you doing here?

EMILY: Therefore, this is half of the emails that the Co-op board sent me about the maintenance.

CLARK: Oh, yeah. Toss it on the pile.

EMILY: You're not paying the maintenance

CLARK: I'm not not paying the maintenance. I just have…things…going on.

EMILY: You kept the apartment -

CLARK: I didn't keep it. You left it.
(rips email in half, tosses it back to her)
My half, your half.

EMILY: ….

CLARK: You couldn't just hit forward.

EMILY: ….

CLARK: You couldn't just drop it in the mail.

EMILY: You don't open your mail.

CLARK: You don't know that.

(Emily opens her bag, dumps a ton of mail at her feet.)

EMILY: I still have my mail box key, too.
What are you doing here Clark?

CLARK: Same shit, different day.

EMILY: Clearly.
You're working?

CLARK: I don't need to work.

EMILY: Use your brain. Write some code. Everyone needs to work. Just for different reasons. Different needs.

CLARK: That's good, write it down. Profess it to your students.

EMILY: …..

CLARK: …..

EMILY: Sam says –

CLARK: You talk to Sam –

EMILY: You know I talk to Sam. She's my sister-in-law.

CLARK: Sister out of law.

EMILY: Not yet.

CLARK: ….

EMILY: I saw them at least three times a week for what, 14 years? I'm just supposed to stop?

(He just looks at her. She gets it.)

CLARK: .....

EMILY: I talk to Sam. Angie and I hang out. We have the girls over.

CLARK: We.

EMILY: ....

CLARK: .....

EMILY: I can't say we?

CLARK: Fine. Say we. Weeweeeweeeweeeweeeeweeeee. All the way fucking home.

EMILY: .....

CLARK: ......

EMILY: You're not paying the maintenance fees.

CLARK: Little things like that get in the way.

EMILY: Little things. Life things. Living things.

Did you burn through all your money?

CLARK: No.

EMILY: Clark.

CLARK: No.

EMILY: Because it was a lot of money.

CLARK: I know. Because I worked for it. And no.

EMILY: ....

CLARK: ....

(Emily starts to clean up.)

Don't don't do that –

EMILY: It's half my place –it's half of my mess. And I want my mess to be unmessed.
....

CLARK: Don't.
Don't.
Don't.

(She dumps a bunch of shit off the couch. Sits.)

EMILY: .....
.....
.....
.....
What are you doing here, Clark?
I talk to Sam, I talk to Angie. They invite me over. Do you want me not to go? Not to say yes?

CLARK: ....

EMILY: Because it's not just me not seeing Lily and Bea. It's the girls losing me too. And I don't think you want to do that to them.
That's not you.

CLARK: I don't want this to even have to be a question you're asking me.

EMILY: Me too. But it is.
....
....
I like to be around the girls. And I hate to be around the girls. I feel like they fill me up and

EMILY (Cont.): they also remind me of what is missing. But it's a little more good than horrendous.

CLARK: Next thing you know you'll be telling me it gets better every day.

EMILY: Look, it –

CLARK: Save your fucking breath.

(he walks off, slams door to bedroom
and then her face collapses.
Bends over trying to catch her breath.
Nauseated.
And up.
He comes back.)

CLARK: There are places where you just say it three times and it becomes true.

I divorce thee –
I divorce thee –
I ---
…
and so on.

EMILY: Where?

CLARK: Somewhere –

CLARK (Cont.): But it has to be me.
Me who says it.
Me who signs it.

EMILY: Then sign it.

CLARK: I'm in, you know that? I'm done.
This is not me holding on. Done. I am.
Are you?

EMILY: What does that mean?

CLARK: You could have just sent your lawyer.

EMILY: I did.

(She digs through the pile of dumped mail and pulls out a large manila envelope)

CLARK: That's a letter.

EMILY: From my lawyer.

CLARK: You could have sent Sam.

EMILY: This is between us.

CLARK: So, there's still an us.

EMILY: Of course, there's still an us. It's just a different us.

How can there not even be an us? And it doesn't get better every day. But some days…

CLARK: ……

EMILY: ……

CLARK: …….

EMILY: What do you need me to do, Clark?

CLARK: What does that mean?

EMILY: It means I know you – you don't come and ask for anything you want. You think asking makes you weak.
So you arrange for it to happen without you asking. You maneuver the world to need to give you what you want.
You don't pay the maintenance or answer my calls or my texts or my emails so I will come to you.
For something.
So I'm asking you.

EMILY (Cont.): What do you need me to do? Please tell me. Please.

CLARK: .....
.....
.....

EMILY: You didn't come to the mediator's office. Twice.
Twice.

CLARK: Mediator. What kind of half-assed person becomes a mediator?

EMILY: ....

CLARK: ....

EMILY: *(re – the papers)* I had these drawn up. They're more than fair. I'm not asking for anything. This place won't be half-mine anymore and I won't have the right to clean up your shit. Sign the papers.

CLARK: ....

EMILY: Sign them Clark. Sign. Sign. Sign. Sign. Sign!

CLARK: .....

EMILY: …..

CLARK: Suck me off and I'll do it.

EMILY: Sweet – talker.
….
….
….
You don't mean that.

CLARK: I do.
I do.

EMILY: ….

CLARK: …..

EMILY: Fine.

(goes to him – pulls his shirt out of his pants, takes down his pants)

CLARK: You're doing this?

EMILY: One more time, what's the difference?

CLARK: Emily.

Emily.
Emily!

EMILY: Just so you know. The tie is broken.
It's broken.
It wasn't. But it is now.
(pulls down his underwear)

CLARK: Get up. Get up. Getupgetupgetup.

EMILY: No.

CLARK: You want it that bad.

EMILY: I want it that bad.

(he pushes her away, harshly
They look at each other.)

FOUR

THE EDGE OF THE SOCCER FIELD. THE EDGE OF THE WORLD.

Samantha. Clark.

SAM: That's it! That's my girl! Down the field!
(tosses Clark sunscreen)
You're pasty.

CLARK: Don't start.

SAM: An observation. Not a comment. I'm glad you're here.
Thank you for being here.
Kick it kick it kick it! Watch out!

CLARK: Did she get slower?

SAM: What?

CLARK: I think of her as being so fast. Used to look away for a sec and she'd be on the other side of the field. Fearless and fast.

SAM: Deal with these.
(She hands him a crate of juice boxes; he stares at them.)
Pull them apart. Stick in ice. You can do it.

She's getting breasts.

CLARK: What?

SAM: Slows them down.

CLARK: She's U10.

SAM: She's U12. She's going on 11. Hips are getting wider. Wind resistance changes. Center of balance is gone. Bellies shifting upwards –
And watch them –They –

SAM (Cont.): Don't run away from the ball, Lily!! Hands hands hands watch your hands. They're protecting themselves. They don't know what to do with all that shit yet.

CLARK: She talks to you about this?

SAM: Nope.

CLARK: And you don't think that's a little pervy - basing game theory on your daughter's teams training bras?

SAM: No. I don't think that's a little pervy.

She's my baby girl. She's just got stuff attached.
You don't remember?

CLARK: What?

SAM: Same for me when I was her age. Exactly.

CLARK: Ugh....

SAM: What?

CLARK: I didn't ever look at you like that.

SAM: Your friends did.

CLARK: I don't need to rewrite that history in my head. I'll keep it the way it was.

(She gives him oranges, knife, cutting board)

SAM: Cut these into quarters.

CLARK: I know what to do.
(cuts)

SAM: You should meet Steven. #14's dad.

CLARK: Why?

SAM: He's developing an app.

CLARK: So we'll be bffs?

SAM: He's a good guy. He's in your field. Quarters.

CLARK: I know.

SAM: These are slices.

CLARK: They're big oranges. Quarters are too big.

SAM: But they like quarters. The way they fit them into their mouths like a smile? That's not a big enough bite.

CLARK: They'll live.

SAM: Come on Lily! Kick it kick it kick it! Get in there!

CLARK: You hated when Dad talked like that.

SAM: ……

CLARK: …..

SAM: Be aggressive, baby!

CLARK: …..

SAM: …..

CLARK: …..

SAM: …..

CLARK: *(making amends)*
Kick it. Kick it. Kickit.

CLARK/SAM: Kickit!

CLARK: Did you see those hands? Where the goddamn ref?

SAM: ….

CLARK: What?

SAM: There you are.

CLARK: ….

SAM: ….

CLARK: I got an email from Mom.

SAM: No. You didn't.

CLARK: The subject heading said "Hi! It's been a long time." And then another one that said "We haven't talked in so long –"

SAM: And the links were for some acai weight loss thing.
I got them too.
They were spam.

CLARK: When I saw them, they didn't feel like spam.

SAM: But they were spam.

SAM (Cont.): And I'm choosing to think they weren't some message from beyond the grave saying she's noticed it's been more than half a decade and I haven't lost the baby weight. I kind of liked them -

CLARK: Of course you did. They allow you to be righteously indignant about her nagging without feeling guilty about not wanting to hang with her for Thanksgiving.

SAM: This is the best I can do at a withering look.

CLARK: …. Sam. It made me think -

SAM: Don't be afraid of the ball!

CLARK: Sam.

SAM: There you go. Hold on to it. Go go go go go go!

CLARK: Sam!

SAM: Goal!

(jumps with joy – Sam turns to high five Clark. He has turned back to cutting the oranges. Cutting. Cutting. Cutting. She watches him.)

SCENE A:

JUST CLARK, IN A PLACE WE CAN'T DEFINE YET

CLARK: I was the kid who taught my dad how to use his Apple II. You can get the whole picture of me from that sentence, right? You're not too wrong. You're not totally right. I was the kid who spent a shitload of time talking girls with my sister - – I was the kid who played baseball, made out with my girlfriend in the dugout, got stoned with my friends. I hit Palo Alto after Penn and was employee seven, cashed out, then employee four, cashed out. You've heard that drill. I loved code more than the cash. It was like a secret universal language. A geek Esperanto. I cashed out, I played hard- I thought, I could always get back in and cash out again. Not so much. I had to do something else. I had to reinvent myself and the moment I saw this woman so excited about whatever the hell she was talking about with her friend that she knocked her coffee all over herself and managed somehow to pull a shirt out of her gym bag and change into it in the middle of the café without missing a beat, I knew I'd be reinventing myself as her husband. I built the Sing it Like App after a really bad night at a

CLARK (Cont.): karaoke bar without earplugs and the Stay at Home Dad App after I found myself cruising You-Tube for diapering instructions. But then – after – I couldn't update it any more and….

(He can't get the words out. Chokes up. Stops.)

FIVE

THE APARTMENT

Emily. Clark.

EMILY: Sam said
Sam said –
You are trying to
…to…Jake…you are trying to email him.

CLARK: Contact.

EMILY: Contact.

CLARK: Communicate. Be with him.

EMILY: Clark.

CLARK: There should be a way.

EMILY: But there isn't -

CLARK: When we were in junior high the idea of walking down Broadway able to talk on the phone was crazy. Fax machines were miraculous and now they're dated. We send a text now and we don't even think about it –

He's not…here. But who knows where the fuck he is.

What if who we are is just energy and bodies were the only way to capture that? But now we can find another way. Technology -

EMILY: You want to turn my son's death into science fiction -

CLARK: Our son.

EMILY: Semantics.

CLARK: When my mom was dying – When my mom was dying and I was in the room she was still my mom lying in front of me. It was still my mom whose hand I was holding. And then her body wasn't her any more and her hand wasn't her anymore but there was something around me. She was around me. It was like she was putting her arms around my neck from behind for a hug. For an everything is going to be all right moment. She was there

CLARK (Cont.): but she wasn't in her body. It was like her body was a mode of communication and it no longer fit her. All I am doing is looking for the new mode of communication.

EMILY: You barely talked to your mother when she was alive. You want to talk to her now that she's dead.

CLARK: There you go –

EMILY: What?

CLARK: De-bunking.

EMILY: Oh come on –

CLARK: People experience something – like a soul – or they feel something nobody else feels or they see something you don't see and -

EMILY: /Hallucinations/ -

CLARK: it's all in their imagin-fucking-ation, says Professor Emily.

EMILY: /are the manifestations of -

CLARK: /You have to kill the joy for everyone else/ – why, why do you have to do that?

EMILY: /Oh my god I swore I'd never have this fight with you again/ and we're off -

CLARK: You are determined to tell them the experiences they enjoy are not real. It's not really love, it's dopamine. You just want to take it away. The great de-bunker takes away the thing that gives them pleasure.

EMILY: You know, I take away the nightmares too. When the devil horns grow out of their heads or their brother looks like he's covered with a flesh-eating virus. I tell them that's not real –

CLARK: You take the magic out of everything.

EMILY: Just because I believe there's a biological basis in how humans respond to various stimuli that people quantify as something other than physiological -

CLARK: People call it feelings – emotions.

EMILY: Semantics. Again.

CLARK: Why can't they just be seeing what they see and feeling what they feel? And then, Professor, you go uptown and enter your hallowed ivy halls and you teach these beautiful post adolescent beings who are all emotion and all feeling that they should disconnect -from the neurons that make them into people – You're just going to sit there and take this?

EMILY: This is how you get when you're mad at me. Reductive. And I'm not going to engage.

CLARK: …

EMILY: ….

CLARK: That is utterly dissatisfying.

EMILY: ….

CLARK: ….
…

EMILY: I'm worried about you.

CLARK: Just turn that little worry neuro-receptor off.

EMILY: Those emails were the voice of someone in Malaysia or China or Nigeria who is working for someone who thinks this is an effective marketing campaign –
Please tell me you know that those emails weren't real. They're not real. That wasn't your mother writing. They weren't from her.

CLARK: Oh no, they weren't from her. But what if they were?
What if they could be real? What if there was a way?

EMILY: There isn't a way.

CLARK: Did you stop loving him?

EMILY: Screw you.

CLARK: Have you stopped loving him?

EMILY: ….
Of course not.

CLARK: Did you stop loving me?

EMILY: ….

CLARK: It's not a trick question.

EMILY: It is a trick question.

CLARK: Did the data centers in your brain stop responding in a love-like manner when I appeared? At the thought of me?

EMILY: No.

CLARK: But they responded to Richard in the same way.

EMILY: No. Yes. No. Not the same.

CLARK: The day I knew we would eventually get divorced – was the day I read the paper you published in the Columbia journal and I realized that I married someone who believes love is a neurological response.

EMILY: Oh please, you still don't believe we're getting divorced.

CLARK: ....

EMILY: You knew then? Because I didn't know until months after Jake died.

CLARK: If love is a scientific amalgam of reception and response - if everything we see, taste, feel, everything in the world is the

CLARK (Cont.): reaction of some neuron, why isn't it possible to believe that love could traverse boundaries that we just haven't been able to cross yet? There's the synapse. There's that gap. Why is it ridiculous to believe that we can't bridge some other gap, a different kind of gap, one that we don't know how to figure out exactly yet but one that transcends the body into a realm that –

EMILY: It's not possible.

CLARK: Some day.
Some day soon if I have something to do with it.
….

EMILY: That neurological response…you were the one who set it off in me. Why you? There's no explanation for that. That was our magic.

CLARK: …..

EMILY: When I'm with you I can't forget myself.

CLARK: …..

EMILY: …..

CLARK: .....

EMILY: What do you have to eat?

CLARK: And.... there you go.

EMILY: Is there food?

CLARK: There's leftovers.

EMILY: From when?

CLARK: From I don't know.
From whenever they were left?

EMILY: Do you have anything with an expiration date that hasn't expired?

CLARK: Beer.

EMILY: What is this?

CLARK: An orange.

EMILY: An orange.
So I won't get scurvy.

CLARK: Can you get out of the fridge?
Get out of the fridge please?

EMILY: It's half my fridge. Still.

CLARK: It's all my food.

Get out of there.
Get out of there.

(she's not going to)

Have you stopped running?

EMILY: A little.

CLARK: You've stopped a little.

EMILY: Why?

CLARK: You look good.

EMILY: Thanks.

CLARK: For a while you – Didn't - I didn't either –But you - you were running too much. You stopped running. You're heartier –

EMILY: Clark.

CLARK: ....

EMILY: ....

CLARK: .....

EMILY: .....

CLARK: ......
How long?

EMILY: ....

CLARK: How long?

EMILY: We're not even telling people yet.

CLARK: We.

EMILY: ....

CLARK: I'm people.

EMILY: No.

CLARK: How could you not tell me?

EMILY: Evidently, I am. Now.

CLARK: .....

EMILY: I didn't know if you would want to
know and the only way I could find out if you
wanted to know would be by asking you if you

EMILY (Cont.): want to know, and then, of course, you would know.

CLARK: ....

EMILY: ....

CLARK: I should have seen it earlier.

EMILY: When was the last time we looked at each other?
When was the last time we were kind to each other?
I'm not even three months.

CLARK: I thought you just got fat.
You're not fat.

EMILY: I'm not.

CLARK: Fucker!

EMILY: ....

CLARK: ....

EMILY: I'm sorry.

CLARK: ....

EMILY: ....

CLARK: You don't want me to have Jake because you have this.

EMILY: No.

CLARK: Because you've just moved on to the next scenario. The unbroken scenario.

EMILY: No –

CLARK: I can't contact him because you're fine –

EMILY: I am not fine –
And you can't contact him because he is not there to be contacted!

CLARK: ...

EMILY: When something devastating and impossible happens there are two choices. Stay where you are or move forward. Hope it didn't happen or move forward. Move forward.

Don't blame me for picking the one you didn't pick.

CLARK: You got to pick?

EMILY: .....

CLARK: .....

EMILY: Do not make me wrong because I am trying to move on and you won't. I am not a bad person for having a life.

CLARK: You only wanted one. That's what you always said. You only wanted one.

EMILY: Yes! I still want that. I want one.

SCENE B:

IN THAT PLACE WE CAN'T DEFINE YET

CLARK: I'm not going to pretend I was the best parent in the world. I lost my patience on a daily, if not hourly basis. I rolled my eyes when he wept because I didn't put his shoes on and then his pants and when he wouldn't put on a jacket or gloves I hauled him outside into the snow and let him get really fucking cold before I handed them over. I gloated when he said he didn't need to study his spelling and got every one wrong on the quiz. Lesson

CLARK (Cont.): learned. So maybe I was a shitty dad in the moment to moment sometimes, but in other moment to moments I was stellar.

I ran out of the middle of the park when he was five with him in my arms and threw myself in front of a full cab at rush hour and begged the people in it to get out so I could get him to the hospital when he fell off the big rock –. I read to him when I didn't want to read to him and I let him kick his feet into my face in the middle of the nights he couldn't sleep anywhere but between us. From the moment he started walking, I can't tell you how many times I'd lose him to find him again. But I'd find him again….

SIX

THE EDGE OF THE SOCCER FIELD. THE EDGE OF THE WORLD

Emily. Samantha.

EMILY: You know I love to be here for the girls.
I couldn't –
With the divorce – or the perpetual divorcing -

EMILY (Cont.): If I had lost them too
If I had lost you and Angie.
Thank you for not taking sides when you probably should have taken sides.
I'm worried about Clark. But I had to ---I'm a terrible person.

SAMANTHA: You're a human person.

EMILY: .....

SAMANTHA: He's a big boy. He can take care of himself.

EMILY: ....

SAMANTHA: I tell myself that if I tell myself that enough, it'll come true.

EMILY: I need coffee.

SAMANTHA: Not supposed to have coffee.

EMILY: That has been made abundantly clear by the sudden disappearance of the beans from the cabinet and my punch cards from my wallet.
As if solidarity makes me need it less.

SAMANTHA: See that girl over there - that's her mom. Number 13's? Her other kid has a personal trainer and he sucks…he just sucks. Not like his sister. But the mom caters snack every week for both teams. Mini hot dogs and baby soy quiches. She said it's because her kid doesn't eat dairy so it's easier for her just to make everything so she knows it's OK. But I saw them buying ice cream at the truck the other day. And that cooler – that's known as the adult cooler. Margaritas.

She wants us to love her. She wants us to love her kid. That much.

EMILY: Does she have coffee?

SAMANTHA: She has lattes. Soy lattes.

EMILY: …..

SAMANTHA: No paper trail. I didn't see a thing. I'll swear.

EMILY: I miss this. When I was dragging my ass to the fields at 8 on Saturdays and bitching about it, I never thought I would miss this.

SAMANTHA: In about ten years I'll still be at this soccer field on Saturday mornings. Only it will be to cheer your kid.

EMILY: Are you sure?

SAMANTHA: As sure as I am they're going to lose if they don't get Lily off the bench.

EMILY: .....

SAMANTHA: .....

EMILY: You're OK with this?

SAMANTHA: Don't I have to be?

EMILY: I wish there was a law.

SAMANTHA: ....

EMILY: ....

SAMANTHA: I'm OK with this.

EMILY: Don't be sure.

Don't be sure of anything.

(They watch the kids play soccer.)

SEVEN

THE APARTMENT

Renee, Clark

RENEE: Love what you've done with the place.

CLARK: You and everyone else. Dump and Compost is coming by to photograph next week.

RENEE: I shouldn't make conversation.

CLARK: You can make whatever you want to make.

RENEE: But that wasn't why you wanted me to come over.
(She moves to sit on the arm of his chair. He moves away.)
....
You'll have things you want to ask me too. Give yourself a minute.

CLARK: The where do I know you from?

RENEE: Yeah.

CLARK: The – you look familiar.
Everyone says that, I bet.

RENEE: Some do. Some don't. Most of them are wrong.

CLARK: ….

RENEE: ….

CLARK: Oh…

RENEE: 17B.

CLARK: This building.

RENEE: Funny how the world works.

CLARK: 17B.

RENEE: I grew up here.

Been living there since just before my mom got sick.

Totally weirding you out.

CLARK: Well, you know, when you answer one of these ads you don't think…well, it's a

CLARK (Cont.): real twist on the whole "won't you be my neighbor?" thing.

RENEE: I usually keep this business out of the neighborhood. I confine myself to the outer boroughs. I don't usually - it's pouring out. It's been pouring all week. I liked the idea of a dry commute.

CLARK: Dubious honor.

RENEE: Usually this is about going out with someone. Not staying in with someone. At least at first. The apartment's great but my mom had some bills. I need a supplement. My real business - I sell things on etsy.

CLARK: Things?

RENEE: One of a kind whatevers I make from whatever I have to make.

CLARK: You're the painted pants lady.

RENEE: What?

CLARK: He called you the painted pants lady.

…

…

This is what you do. Your survival job?

RENEE: I started in art school just to help myself out sometimes. I trust you're not going to tell anyone.

CLARK: Why do you trust?

RENEE: I don't see you in the elevator any more. I see a lot of delivery guys.
I guess I wanted to know how you were…
You hear things. The big things. That kind of news travels in the building, but the little stuff, the daily stuff, what happens after doesn't.
We're not friends, we're New
York neighbors, we co-exist. When my mom and I moved in here – they took back the building. It was like we were homesteading. People watched out for each other. Things change.

I thought it couldn't be a coincidence you went for me. I guess this was to satisfy my curiosity.
I didn't think you'd care.
I thought it could be a good thing.

CLARK: I don't do this a lot.

RENEE: No.
It didn't seem like that. Too many emails back and forth.

RENEE (Cont.): I could have just played it through. But since I'd already sent you my photo - you were going to recognize me. If not here then in the elevator. Here is much better than the elevator.

CLARK: You're not going to ask about him?

RENEE: I know about him. I know enough. Unless you want me to.
(her eyes keep going to strange little device on the table)
That's not…what is that?
Is that it?

CLARK: You know what I'm doing?

RENEE: Yeah, well, you told Juan Carlo what you were doing when he brought up your packages. Man's got a mouth on him. So then, people talk – about what you're doing. What you're not doing.

It's not like you're hanging out a shingle and reading tarot cards – but some people feel like you're…inviting…something. They don't want to push you to leave because they don't want to be the kind of people who would do that to someone who has gone through what you've gone through, but on the other hand

RENEE (Cont.): there are rules and they follow the rules. But on the other hand –

CLARK: There's another hand?

RENEE: There's always another hand.
…

Is that it?

CLARK: You can touch it.
(she hesitates)
It's not it yet. But I think this may be the one. It won't bite.
(She still doesn't touch it)
There's what we see, right? You see me, you see the street, the stars, the sky. Your body processes that. Our eyes do it – we use visible light, which is one type of electromagnetic radiation. There are other kinds of EM radiation we can't see with our eyes but we can detect them in different ways – with those dishes- you've seen pictures of them – huge radio arrays, each of them like 80 feet across, they weigh hundreds of tons, they'll have dozens of them spread out in the desert, trying to listen to space.

RENEE: Is this the cereal box version of that?

CLARK: No – it's my buddy's prototype -

RENEE: ....

CLARK: He works at the lab out at San Augustin where they're trying to make a very small, very large array. Been cracking his ass at it as long as I've known him. His idea was to make phased magnetic fields to create an extremely high resolution lens...Anyway this thing is so incredibly sensitive he thought it would be able to measure frequencies from the ends of the universe. And this gives off readings, but once he analyzed the data he realized it's not receiving the EM waves he wanted to read at all. The waves it's detecting, they are nothing like anything we've ever seen before. Which is great!

RENEE: OK –

CLARK: Because my theory – my theory is that maybe it's detecting something else. Something beyond the electromagnetic spectrum we think we know. The energy of the person who has died. Their soul. And if that's it, and if I can code the shit out of this, which I think I can, maybe that's the first step in communicating with someone who just doesn't have a body anymore.

RENEE: ….

CLARK: …

RENEE: Usually, when I…meet new people, we don't get much deeper than talking about the weather.

CLARK: What happened when your mother died?

RENEE: She died.

CLARK: But what happened?

RENEE: I don't know. I wasn't there.
I was out.
She wanted me to go out. Have fun. Fuck the deathwatch.
So I was on deathwatch, but not watching.
I was out.

CLARK: And when you came back?

RENEE: I don't -

CLARK: When you came back –

RENEE: When I came back….

(she shrugs)

SCENE D

WE SEE WHAT THAT PLACE WITHOUT DEFINITION IS – IT IS CLARK RECORDING HIMSELF ON HIS LAPTOP

Emily - elsewhere - watching the recording on her laptop.

CLARK: Hi – I am Clark and I miss my son. I'm sure there's someone you miss. Someone you thought earth would prevent you from speaking to until you die.

I am an app developer and software savant on a mission to contact those who are not currently contactable by conventional means. We always talk about the things you didn't get to say to someone. I am developing the technology so you can say those things and feel heard. So you can be the two of you again.

Unbelievable, you say? But look around you. There are so many things part of our every day world right now that would have been unthinkable until recently. Organ transplants, a phone you can carry down the street, texting.

CLARK (Cont.): I miss my son. I want to talk to him. I want to know how he is. I want to feel the way he sounded so wise and so six, seven, eight, nine, ten years old at the same time. I want to fight with him over whether or not I am the boss of him.

Sometimes I feel him in the air around me as if he is trying to break through. What if I can help him break through? What if I can break through to him? What if I can help you break through to yours? That's why I'm putting this out there and looking for backers.

Do I know I can make this happen? In my heart. Yes.
Why can't I?

EIGHT

THE APARTMENT

Emily, Clark

EMILY: @thespeedofJake? Really?

CLARK: When I asked why you still had a key -

EMILY: If you didn't want to me come over you wouldn't have sent me the link in the middle of the night.

CLARK: …

EMILY: I'm trying to understand. I am.
….

CLARK: …

EMILY: I get the theory, Clark. I get the longing. I get the missing. I get wanting to talk to him. To be with him. I don't get the practice. I don't get the doing this. I might be a scientist but I'm always a parent first. I don't get inviting people in – to our pain –

CLARK: to the possibility –

Don't you want to talk to him?

When Jake was in there you talked to him all the time. He wasn't human yet, he wasn't a person but you said you felt a connection.

EMILY: That's different. That's totally different.

CLARK: I still feel a connection.

EMILY: Of course you do - If I could have him back the way he was – sure. But even if you could do what you're trying to do it wouldn't be that.

CLARK: But with that connection, that feeling, I think I can - Let me - show you what I've done so far.

EMILY: No.

CLARK: You're scared.

EMILY: I'm hurt. You're making him into an APP!

CLARK: It's not an app.

EMILY/CLARK: Semantics.

EMILY: You need to let him go, Clark.

CLARK: Why?

EMILY: Because that's what people do.

CLARK: You know, I haven't felt this good in a long time. I haven't felt this purposeful in – I had forgotten.

CLARK (Cont.): You're the one who wanted
me to work at something again.
No one knows what dead is.
We know what dead isn't. But what is alive?
Is it a feeling? Is it a state?
I am attempting something that's just at the
edge of possibly believable. This is being alive.

Some people might call it faith. And that's
why the kickstarter. Because I need to feel
someone else's faith. In me.

EMILY: I never didn't have faith in you.

CLARK: You left.

EMILY: I survived.

CLARK: And I'm surviving by doing what you
told me to do for years. Get a goal to make me
feel purposeful. An outside interest that
garners a different kind of attention. Positive
attention rather than dad of the dead kid
attention.

EMILY: You're still the dad of the dead kid.
Even if you make this thing work, which you
won't, because you can't, you never won't be
the dad of the dead kid.
That doesn't stop.

EMILY (Cont.): You think I think *(her belly)* this will stop it? I'll just be the mom who had another kid who died. Always.

I wouldn't want to talk to him in the ether where I don't know where he is or I can't touch him. He's not going to grow up. He's not going to grow older -

(Emily bends over as if she is going to throw up.)

CLARK: Don't puke in my apartment.

EMILY: Our apartment.

CLARK: I'm not going to hold back your hair. I'm not going to clean it up.

EMILY: *(regains composure)*
Yeah, you would. You know you would.

You think that could be him? That's not his skin. That's not his body. That's not him running down the field, snuggling up to us at night. You can't capture his essence in a way that's meaningful.

(Emily walks out of the room to Jake's bedroom –)

CLARK: There's no faith in me there.

(-she comes back to Clark with a huge sketchbook filled with drawings)

EMILY: How can you capture the boy who was making this?
This wasn't about some pansy-assed girl eating sweets, staying remarkably slim and waiting for her prince to come, a boy writing a story about the wolf – the she wolf who got turned into a princess

CLARK: - which was sometimes a bit of a problem because of the hairiness factor –

EMILY: and the tough part of trying to chew with her mouth closed.

CLARK: Werewolf princess.

EMILY: But it wasn't a full moon thing. It was a wake up and your body has moved on without you thing. ... Hello puberty.

CLARK: He was 10, Em.

EMILY: He was trying to make sense of the random hairs -

CLARK: He didn't have –
(She holds up three fingers) He showed you -

EMILY: Of course he did. I was his mom.

CLARK: But –

EMILY: You got to talk to him about other things. That part just ended up being mine.

CLARK: You never told me.

EMILY: It just didn't –

CLARK: Not even after –

EMILY: After – everything that was after was after.

CLARK: .....

EMILY: ....

CLARK: Why wouldn't you tell me that?

EMILY: I wasn't keeping it for myself. There were things I kept for myself - I got a bill for the remainder of the bar mitzvah fees. You know what it was like to get that? They make you pick a date in the fourth grade, you'd think they'd have an office protocol to make sure shit like that didn't fall through the cracks. The camp brochures. The catalogues. Those

EMILY (Cont.): automated calls about the baseball schedule and swim team. Those I kept for myself. I didn't want them. But those were not moments you would have wanted to share.

CLARK: There's nothing about Jake I wouldn't have wanted to share.

EMILY: I was trying to protect you. I was.

Have you turned it on yet?

CLARK: What?

EMILY: Have you turned it on?

CLARK: It's on.

EMILY: ….
…
…it's on…

CLARK: It's always on. It's waiting. I keep fine-tuning.

EMILY: It's waiting? Just like you….
…
….
….
And –

CLARK: Just not yet.

EMILY: …

CLARK: ….

EMILY: …

CLARK: I'm not the only one who wants to know. I'm not the only one who believes in me. In the time you've been here I've gone from 11 to 59 backers.

EMILY: What's the difference? Let's say I have faith. Let's say you can do this. I'm asking you not to.

CLARK: You let go, Em. You let go of this. Let me be.

(Emily takes the graphic novel. Goes.)

NINE

THE APARTMENT

Richard, Clark

CLARK: And you found me how?

RICHARD: It's not hard to find anyone these days.

CLARK: In my understanding, most people just press the donate now button. Or they call first. I'm not even going to say I would have cleaned up.

RICHARD: It doesn't bother me.

CLARK: You're the only one.

RICHARD: Kind of comforting.

CLARK: I'm not a hoarder.

RICHARD: Just a pig –

CLARK: ....

RICHARD: You're thinking about bigger things. I have a cousin – an artist – older woman, more my mom's age, and whenever she was in the thick of it she'd reek, no time to shower, no time to find anything, no time to put something away. Pay a bill. And maybe it looked like she had time because technically there was time - it seemed like she was doing nothing. There was a whole lot of staring at walls, a whole lot of long walks and sleepless

RICHARD (Cont.): nights and then she'd be in the thick of it, looking like a madwoman by the end of each sculpture. And then after the end, all the detritus would be cleared out, everything arranged, things shined until she was ready to begin again.

CLARK: You do this often?

RICHARD: Show up uninvited? No.

CLARK: Inquire about becoming a project's major funder.

RICHARD: Oh. No. Not that kind of money. Would be cool, though, wouldn't it, to fund people's dreams arbitrarily.

CLARK: Arbitrarily?

RICHARD: Well, you know, scrolling through the sites – this project looks interesting. What about that project? Those speakers look cool and they only have three hours left to hit their goal. I can't believe that shirt doesn't need to be washed.

CLARK: You don't seem like an arbitrary guy.

RICHARD: What makes you say that?

CLARK: I think you think about everything you do. Those shoes are deliberate. What time you showed up here was thought out.

...

It's a compliment.

...

I doubt the word whatever has ever come out of your mouth.

You picked my campaign for a reason. Not because you rolled the dice.

RICHARD: I brought beer. You want a beer?

CLARK: You brought beer.

RICHARD: I don't like to show up without something.

(holds one out. Clark takes it.)

Hot day, outside.

CLARK: Is it?

RICHARD: One of those days the air shimmers in October.

CLARK: So you came to be convinced.

RICHARD: ....

CLARK: Who are you missing?

RICHARD: What?

CLARK: The kickstarter.
There must be someone you're missing.

RICHARD: Oh.
...

CLARK: ....

RICHARD: My fiancé.

CLARK: ....

RICHARD: ....

CLARK: ....

Emily.

RICHARD: What?

CLARK: Did something happen to Emily?
What is it?
What happened? Is she OK?

RICHARD: No no no no no no.
She's fine.
She's fine.
Fine

CLARK: ….

RICHARD: How did you know?

CLARK: It's not hard to find anyone these days.

You had no fucking right to freak me out like that.

RICHARD: That wasn't what I was trying to do.

CLARK: You said you were missing her.

RICHARD: I didn't know you knew it was me.

CLARK: Most people fucking call.

RICHARD: You would have let me in?

CLARK: Most people who should stay away stay away.
….

CLARK (Cont.): ….

She sent you?

RICHARD: I sent me.
…
I am missing her. There's part of her that's missing.
Maybe she does need this -- I don't know. You know her – she'll
hide behind the technical terms and categorize it all in a logical way, but when it comes down to Jake I know behind it all there's a chasm of longing and questions and…longing under her resolve to move on.

And I have to say I wonder, I do wonder if this would – could be…

Look, you want to be part of our lives, be part of our lives. You're always going to have a piece of her so I will welcome you. I will. I know it's not what you want but it's what's here.

If this is what she needs….

If you're what she needs…

I want her to have what she needs.

CLARK: Why?

RICHARD: Why?

CLARK: Why?

RICHARD: So I can have what I need.

CLARK: .....

RICHARD: .....

TEN

THE APARTMENT

Clark, Renee. On the couch. She's making him laugh.

RENEE: No one says that. They don't say that.

CLARK: Salad days....

RENEE: That's like some phrase people reminisced with in the 20s.
That's a new diet book.

CLARK: I did not make it up.

RENEE: You should have because you're the only one on this earth who ever uses it.

And why would they call it salad days any ways? I'm looking back fondly and I'm thinking about bib lettuce, carrots, cucumber slices. Makes no sense.

CLARK: Well, there you go. Welcome to the English language.

RENEE: You made me hungry.

CLARK: Talking about salad days.

RENEE: Doesn't take much…You gonna feed me?

CLARK: We can order.

RENEE: You don't have any food.

You don't cook?
You want me gone?

CLARK: ….

RENEE: …..

CLARK: ….

RENEE: OK. I'm gone.

CLARK: Don't.

RENEE: Don't what?

CLARK: There's salmon. In the freezer. I think.

RENEE: How long has it been in there?

CLARK: It's frozen.

RENEE: So?

CLARK: It's like time has stopped. It was on sale. I knew I was never going to cook it when I bought it. But I thought buying it, buying it would prove that I was making an attempt.

RENEE: When you know up front you're faking it who the hell else do you think you're going to convince?

CLARK: Do you want it?

RENEE: You don't have anything else in there? No mac and cheese? No Salisbury steak.

CLARK: Who eats that?

RENEE: I did. In my salad days.

My blood sugar's low.

CLARK: I have menus.

RENEE: Menus?

CLARK: Lots and lots of menus.

RENEE: You ever gonna clean this? Doesn't inspire confidence, you know.

CLARK: It'll just get dirty.

RENEE: If you let it.

CLARK: Nope. Does it on its own.

RENEE: Don't give me that.

CLARK: It just flourishes overnight. Like weeds.

RENEE: Styrofoam weeds. Aluminum weeds.

CLARK: Believe me or don't.

RENEE: That smell isn't natural.

CLARK: What smell? There's a smell?

RENEE: BBQ rot. Pepperoni compost.
(she picks takeout boxes out of the pile as an example)

CLARK: I don't smell anything.

RENEE: Kung Pao crap.

CLARK: I just - could you stop that -

Just - just don't. Don't. I can't touch that stuff. I know the drill. One little area at a time. You can't avoid those shows where they make over someone's life just by throwing out their crap. There's always a big freeing emotional moment before the third commercial break and the cliffhanger – will they or will they not get rid of their shit? But I start unpiling those piles, clean out the top layer of takeout containers to the next layer of last month's magazines and maybe some shirts with holes and behind that shale of last February to the August before there is unopened mail, a shit-load of catalogues from GAP kids and City Sports and summer programs with wizarding camps and behind that are the fluttering layers of condolence cards from people who used to write cards. And the layer behind that is a

CLARK (Cont.): layer that still bears a little impression of his touch where his greasy popcorn fingers couldn't wait to open the book or where the mud from his cleats clumped at the edge of the carpet or the wet towel he left on the floor that under all that, it could still be damp. That's his damp. And as much as anyone might think – get rid of it and I will be freed – I can't do that, I can't.

That feeling I get when I think about him, the feeling you get when you think about your mom, the way you talk about her – That's what I need to be able to capture. It's like it's a fingerprint she left on you. And I think if I can quantify that, I can use that fingerprint to define her greater resonance. And once I detect that, I can work on decoding –

RENEE: You knew it was me.

CLARK: What?

RENEE: All the time, when you…found me. You knew it was me.

CLARK: I knew your mom. I liked your mom. Hell, I want to talk to her again.

RENEE: You could have just said –

CLARK: Would you have –

RENEE: You could have just told me –

CLARK: I didn't think –

RENEE: You didn't need to trick me –

CLARK: This is tricking you? Paying you to just hang out here and eat my non-existent food?

Look -- Crazy guy in 12B starts asking if I want to talk to my dead mom – as if I don't have enough troubles with the co-op board.

The building was different after she was gone.

RENEE: I know that. I feel that -

(Renee gets her things to go)

CLARK: What are you doing?

RENEE: I don't want this –
Complications! Hope!
It's hard enough. You know that. It's hard enough.

CLARK: .....

RENEE: …..

CLARK: I didn't mean -

RENEE: I'm sure you didn't –

CLARK: I thought getting to know you this way –

RENEE: Getting to know me? Like I'm a lab rabbit?

CLARK: I'm never going to think of the right words for this –

(He pulls out money)

RENEE: What's that for?

CLARK: I just don't want you to go.

I read you wrong? I thought this was something you wanted. Why you've come back since that first time. All signs pointed…here.

RENEE: I thought this was a gig. A weird gig. An easy gig but -

CLARK: Really?

RENEE: ….

(He throws down his wallet.)

CLARK: I think it could be helpful to me if you would be here. More.

RENEE: ….

CLARK: ….

RENEE: You'd think – sitting with her all the time for the last few months, living with her for the last seven years, you'd think I wouldn't have any questions left ...but every day there's something.

(she stays.)

ELEVEN

THE APARTMENT

Clark, Richard

RICHARD: How close are you?

CLARK: Close.

RICHARD: Do you have a beta?

CLARK: I'm working on it.

RICHARD: Have you distinguished anything, anything at all? –

CLARK: I'm working on it!

RICHARD: You said you knew what you were doing.

CLARK: I did -

RICHARD: But you don't –

CLARK: I know what I'm doing, I just don't know how to do it yet.
This isn't simple.

RICHARD: I wouldn't think it would be.

CLARK: I'm looking for something distinctive in the patterns. It has to be singular – like its own genetic code. And then I can –

RICHARD: Why did you ask people for money?

CLARK: What?

RICHARD: You charged them –

CLARK: Minimally.

RICHARD: But still –

CLARK: 50 bucks –

RICHARD: 1729 people. 50 dollars each.

CLARK: They'll be getting more than their money's worth.

RICHARD: When?

CLARK: What?

RICHARD: When?

CLARK: ….

RICHARD: You've missed your deadline. Deadlines.

CLARK: I know.

RICHARD: You said you were going to deliver by -

CLARK: I know - and maybe, if you'd stop coming around, gnawing at me, I'd actually get it done.

RICHARD: You're the one who opens your goddamn door.

CLARK: Well it's not for the beer.

RICHARD: ….

Eighty-six thousand, four hundred and fifty dollars.

CLARK: It's not about the money.

RICHARD: 1729 backers. 1729 people.

CLARK: I know they're people. I need them to believe in me.

RICHARD: What are you, Tinkerbell?

CLARK: And they need me just as much.

RICHARD: Tinkerbell with a God complex.

CLARK: Better than therapy. Better drowning in a case of wine every couple of weeks.

RICHARD: Your kickstarter as your own personal support group.

CLARK: That's the only way to make it work. I'm going to need people to test it out for me. People I don't know. People I can't read –

RICHARD: People who by now, probably think you're full of shit.

CLARK: What?

RICHARD: They're thinking you're no better than the guy pushing the Ouija board to yes. No better than the jerk cold reading a grieving widow. You tracked me down - You know how to research people – why don't you just send them an email that sounds like it's from their dead cousin or boyfriend and be done with it?

CLARK: Because that's not who I am -

RICHARD: You promised them something and you've given them nothing.

CLARK: I've given them hope.
You know those people whose kids go missing and everyone assumes they're dead and hopes they would go find a body for closure. Well I envy them because they have hope. And I didn't have hope. And now I do.
I'm going to deliver.

CLARK (Cont.): I'm giving them something. I'm giving them hope.

RICHARD: And what happens when you don't deliver?

CLARK: ….

RICHARD: Emily only has doubts because of you.

CLARK: What?

RICHARD: You hold on to your belief that because of what she does for a living she doesn't feel anything. But it's not true. And you know it's not true. It's just where you guys landed yourselves in the pain.

I walk into the bedroom she's got that t-shirt Jake used to sleep in and she's just holding it like it will have answers. There're no answers. And she used to know she wasn't going to get any answers and she had made her peace with that. An uneasy crackling peace. But now, now she's starting to want answers again. She's starting to need them again.

CLARK: ….

RICHARD: ….

CLARK: I'm afraid if I stop missing him it will be like he didn't exist.

RICHARD: That can't happen. He's always going to be –

CLARK: Please don't spew the bullshit party line that you know nothing about.

RICHARD: You're right. I can't know it. All I can do is live in fear it will happen to us. That it will happen to her again. I don't want it to happen to her again. And all of these people, I can't help but think - they don't deserve losing someone any more than you and Emily deserved what happened to you.

You've resurrected her grief. And maybe their's too.

CLARK: That's not what –

RICHARD: That's what you've done.

CLARK: It's supposed to be about possibility. Not about…

RICHARD: ….

RICHARD (Cont.): ….

Maybe you don't think that's what you meant to do.

CLARK: But that –

RICHARD: That's what you've done.

(Richard leaves Clark alone.)

TWELVE

THE APARTMENT

Emily, obviously pregnant. Clark

EMILY: I knew you'd be up. And I'm not going to sleep.
I don't know how I can feel so lonely when I'm not alone at all.
I was trying to calculate the time difference to all the places I know people in this country. Early/late in Seattle so no Jackie. Middle of the night in Chicago – that rules out all of my cousins. Everyone international is at work. What's the point of free long distance if there's no one to call?

EMILY (Cont.): You need to make an insomniac app. Get in touch with whoever's awake.

CLARK: This isn't a good time.

EMILY: I'll just sit on the couch. Shut up. You work.

All those nights we'd sit here praying no one in the building – in the city – would make a sound for the 23 minutes it would take him to fall asleep or the clock would reset again.

CLARK: Emily –

EMILY: Shhhhhhh –

CLARK: I –

EMILY: Clock starting again.

CLARK: ….

EMILY: Shhhhhhh
(whispering)
And you'd whisper…"What do you think? Do you think now? Now??"

CLARK: …And you'd whisper "Quiet quiet quiet quiet quiet" really loud.

EMILY: And you'd say "Was that him?" And the clock would reset. Again.

CLARK: And you'd whisper "I can't fall asleep until he falls asleep."

EMILY: And you'd whisper, "I want to talk to you, really talk to you."
Shhhhhhh
Shhhhhhhhh
Shhhhhhhhhhh
And he'd give out that big sigh/snore and his breath on the monitor would change and we'd look at each other with this big sigh of relief -

CLARK: And you'd say "Fuck me now."

EMILY: Did I ever really say fuck me now?

CLARK: You did.

EMILY: I don't know that person any more.
All these moments that at the moment I was sure I'd never forget –
Gone.
…

EMILY (Cont.): …

Fuck me now.

CLARK: ….

EMILY: …..

CLARK: ….

EMILY: …..

(Renee walks out of the bedroom, sleepy to grab a bottle of water, gets it. Goes back.)

That's my shirt.

CLARK: ….

EMILY: ….

CLARK: ….

EMILY: …..

Who is that?

CLARK: Grief counselor.

EMILY: Where did you find her?

CLARK: Craigslist.

EMILY: That's good. You're reaching out.
That's good.

CLARK: Did you mean that?

EMILY: Yes. It's my shirt.

CLARK: .....

EMILY: I think I did.

CLARK: ....

EMILY: ....

CLARK: ....

EMILY: ....

CLARK: I signed.

EMILY: You did?

CLARK: Baby warming present.
They're in the mail.

EMILY: OK.
...

EMILY (Cont.): …

CLARK: What?

EMILY: I thought –

CLARK: ….

EMILY: I don't know. Somehow, I thought. I thought we'd do it together.

CLARK: …

EMILY: …

CLARK: It's done.

EMILY: …
….

OK.

OK.
OK.
OK.
OK.

(He goes into the bedroom.
Emily goes to his laptop.
Angles it so it catches her face – hits record.)

EMILY: I…I… I was –
Hi Clark –

The video of Emily continues as she leaves the room and Clark comes in to watch this video of Emily on his laptop.

EMILY: I…I was …
Hi Clark –

I was a mother, and then not, and now I'm an almost mom again. During the not years I did not know how to answer the questions – are you married? Do you have kids? I do not like to lie but I found myself breathing lies constantly and then I found not talking to people easier than talking to people and then that meant that I was no longer breathing lies but I also wasn't breathing the truth. I was not breathing at all. I am so full of missing. I am here, I am old. I never thought I would get to old. I thought I would finish myself off long before this. In the mornings I would rise out of sleep with the dreamy intention of slicing the blade into each wrist but couldn't manage more than a harsh scratch.

I was not brave.

If I had been brave I would have taken the glorious flame and burst out of this world into

EMILY (Cont.): whatever else there is. I snuck on. I begged for someone to lift the pain and when it did I….I….I…just kept going on. And now I am done. Am I done? Clark – am I done?

I begged for someone to lift the pain and when it did I….I….I…just kept going on. And now I am done. Am I done? Clark – am I done?

Emily leaves him her key to the apartment.

The video ends.

Clark picks up the key from his desk.

The device vibrates sharply. Loudly. Three times. Clark stops. Looks at it.

THIRTEEN

THE APARTMENT

Clark, Sam. Clark is deep in his work.

SAM: I don't know, you signed the divorce papers, you've got that Craigslist girl.

(Sam takes off her coat to reveal she's wearing a hideous yellow and black striped soccer ref uniform).

SAM (Cont.): I thought maybe…there was the slightest possibility of –

CLARK: Of what?

(Clark looks up, sees what she's wearing.)
….

SAM: What?

CLARK: …..

SAM: All the parents have to volunteer.

CLARK: You couldn't bake?

SAM: Angie likes it.

CLARK: No, she does not.

SAM: I could tell you the myriad of ways she likes it…

(but he's back into his work)

Take a break with me.

CLARK: I'm on to something here. There was a noticeable detection and I'm on the cusp of deciphering …

(back into the work)

SAM: …

CLARK: ….

SAM: Can you stop for just a minute?

CLARK: ….

SAM: Angie has to file for bankruptcy for her business.

CLARK: What?

SAM: It's tanked. It's over. It's done. She's been working 24/7 for the last eight months since they had to recall –

CLARK: There was a recall?

SAM: We're lucky no one got hurt. We're lucky…But - it's over.

CLARK: You should have told me.

SAM: Like I was going to tell you. We'll be fine.

CLARK: You need money. I got money.

SAM: We'll be fine. It's just -

CLARK: OK. Good. Problem solved.

(he goes back to work)

SAM: ….

CLARK: ….

SAM: What happens if something happens to me? To me and to Angie? Who will have the girls if something happens to me and to Angie?

CLARK: Angie's family.

SAM: Not an option and you know it.

CLARK: I can't play the "if" game right now, Sam.

SAM: You are playing the "if" game. If you can contact Jake, maybe you can see him, if you can see him maybe you can manifest him, if you can manifest him maybe you can touch him, if

SAM (Cont.): you can touch him maybe you'll come home one night and he'll be sleeping in his bed and maybe you can make it so none of this ever happened.
It's supposed to be you. You're the one I'm supposed to be able to count on – to at least listen.
There are living breathing people who for some reason love you who –

CLARK: Can't you see? Can't you see what I'm doing here?

SAM: No! I can't!

FOURTEEN

THE EDGE OF THE SOCCER FIELD

Richard, Emily. Emily holding a wrapped gift.

RICHARD: So we just watch.
Every week.

EMILY: Twice a week.

RICHARD: Twice.

EMILY: Modern parenting.

RICHARD: But I won't have to wear that yellow shirt?

EMILY: Here's the thing – by then you'll want to wear that yellow shirt.

RICHARD: What about golf?

EMILY: Golf won't be so important. Or working out. Or movies in theatres.

RICHARD: What about brunch?

(She gives him a look.)

EMILY: Go Lily go go go go go go!

(Sam comes up on them from behind to cheer Lily on.)

SAM: Go go go go go go!

EMILY: Oh -

SAM: That goalie never lets one past her.

EMILY: Hi.

SAM: Hi.

RICHARD: Hi.

SAM: Hi.

EMILY: We just stopped by for a latte.

SAM: .....

(she holds out the gift)

EMILY: I'm sorry we didn't show up to the party –

SAM: It's OK.

EMILY: We wanted to come -

SAM: It's OK.

EMILY: But then I thought –

SAM: It's in the past – I just rearranged the place cards.

RICHARD: There were place cards?

SAM: Oh, there was significant party planning going on there.   You don't turn 11 every day.

EMILY: You're his sister. You're his. And, right now -

SAM: Yeah, well, he didn't come either.

RICHARD: And that surprised you?

EMILY: Richard -

SAM: Probably invited you more for me than for Lily anyway – at 11 the grownups are just there to slice cake and clean up – so my bad for counting on you for that too -
Foul foul foulfoulfoul. Oh, come on!

EMILY: We wanted to be there, for Lily. I meant to be there. I thought I was coming. But I just couldn't do it.

SAM: That's O.K.

EMILY: Really?

SAM: Absolutely.

(Sam and Emily look at each other. Richard catches what's going on on the field)
RICHARD: Oh my god. Oh my god. Goal!

EMILY: We should go.

RICHARD: We should?

EMILY: *(to Sam)* Should we?

SAM: Do what's good for you. You always do anyway.

EMILY: Whoa.

RICHARD: What's going on?

SAM: Just watching my kid play soccer.

EMILY: All right. All right then.

(they go -)

SAM: Let me ask you something.

(they stop)

That lecture you basically forced me to come to. Do you still feel that way?

EMILY: Which lecture –

SAM: In the beginning of me and Angie. - I didn't understand it then, god, Angie and I were intoxicated with each other and I felt like

SAM (Cont.): you invited me to say, love is just biochemical, it isn't real, get over yourself.

EMILY: I didn't mean to -

SAM: Because it makes me wonder then - why would you keep coming to see me? Why would you take the girls out? Why the hell Richard and this baby, this new baby –

EMILY: Sam –

SAM: If love is those things you say, if our emotions are just about how our neurons are firing, how can you claim you were sad when Jake died?

EMILY: Sam –

SAM: How can you claim grief?

EMILY: You think I'm claiming to grieve…

SAM: I don't know - You and this new beautiful life, that's not hard but an 11 year old's birthday party is? If you're such a great fucking scientist why can't you help Clark? Help him or help me help him. Or even just help me. Tell me what chemical reaction is responsible for feeling lost and helpless. Solve

SAM (Cont.): these feelings or what are you fucking worth anyway?

EMILY: You said you were OK with this.

SAM: Well I'm not. I'm not OK with this. I'm not OK with anything.

EMILY: Well neither am I!

SAM: …..

EMILY: ….

SAM: ….

EMILY: I tried with him. You know I tried -

SAM: I don't know what to do any more.

(Emily goes to Sam and puts her arms around her, holding her.)

EMILY: Neither do I.

FIFTEEN

THE APARTMENT

Clark, Renee

CLARK: It's a little buggy. It didn't come out to what I thought would be him. I worked it every possible way I could think of –

RENEE: You didn't find him?

CLARK: It detected something.

RENEE: But not him.

CLARK: It was something.
Then I thought, you've been here so much. Maybe the fingerprints are a little confused, the resonance –

RENEE: It doesn't work.

CLARK: Yet.
I'm not going to let one false positive stop me –
That's where you come in.

RENEE: Me?

CLARK: You. Your mom.

RENEE: I talk to her anyway, you know. All the time. All the time. Chatter away at her in the kitchen.

CLARK: That's not the same thing.

RENEE: Neither is this!

CLARK: But you told me – you have questions…unending questions…You ask the questions and I decode the answers.

RENEE: Maybe in the natural progression of things –

CLARK: What?

RENEE: Unanswered questions are just supposed to go unanswered.

CLARK: I can't believe that.

RENEE: The thing is I miss her. I miss the sound of her voice. And you can't give me that. She's gone.

(Clark pulls out his wallet and cash)

RENEE: Don't. I don't want that.
CLARK: Please.
Please!

(He sinks down on to the couch).

RENEE: I know – the world's not the same.
And the world's never going to be the same.

(She leaves him.)

SIXTEEN

THE APARTMENT

Emily is huge.

EMILY: I'm huge. I know.
I know you don't want me here…

CLARK: …..

EMILY: I know. You're working.

CLARK: …

EMILY: I'll go.

CLARK: ……

EMILY: ….

CLARK: ….

EMILY: I wasn't planning on coming here. I was downtown. On eighth. I was looking for shoes. My feet don't fit into anything any more and I'm wearing flip flops and it's going to snow tomorrow. I need shoes.

And the girl who is helping me put them on, you can tell that she doesn't think this is part of her job description, she should just be getting the box in the next size and I should be putting them on but I can't get them on and she's lacing one up, kind of pissed, and I was thinking how annoyed I'd get at Jake because he wouldn't tie his shoes when they got untied. Life was just too interesting to stop and do it and what annoyed me wasn't so much that he didn't tie them than that I was having to be on him about tying them, that I was always worried he'd trip and hurt himself and I resented thinking that because it took away from me being able to enjoy whatever we were in the middle of, being worried he was going to get hurt, I was always worried that he was going to get hurt.

And this girl puts the other shoe on me and ties it and I stand up and my water breaks and it -

CLARK: -No -

EMILY: Really fucking soaks her.

(and they laugh)

I couldn't have aimed better.
...

I can't do this. I can't live with thinking I might lose him every day.

CLARK: Emily -

EMILY: Sam said you said you had detected something and I know she thinks you've gone over the edge and I was thinking you've gone over the edge but what if…??

So my water breaks and I end up here because maybe, maybe you could tell me what it was that you detected and that would answer –

17 days. 17 days of Jake in the hospital. Of trying to reach him. Of saying "I know you were riding, just riding, and your tire blowing out was not your fault. I know baby. I know you were wearing your helmet, I know you did everything right, and still everything we taught you to do didn't make a fuck's worth of difference".

(contraction)

CLARK: Emily
I'm going to call Richard –

EMILY: No no no no no -
....

I'm not letting him out.

CLARK: What?

EMILY: I can't. I can't.

CLARK: Emily.

EMILY: I can't let him out into this world. Not unless Jake…not unless I know he's O.K. And that everything will be O.K.

CLARK: Everything will be –

EMILY: It's not for you to tell me. It's for him to tell me!
I'm not letting him out. I'm not leaving here. I can't.

CLARK: Emily –

EMILY: I need Jake.

CLARK: I know.
You know I know.

EMILY: I can't I can't I can't I can't I can't....

CLARK: ....

You have to.

...

EMILY: .....

CLARK: We have to.

(He takes her hand. She lets him lead her out of the apartment)

SEVENTEEN

THE APARTMENT

Clark enters.

He surveys the room.

He pulls Jake's soccer ball out from the pile. Holds it lightly in his hands for a moment.

He puts it down. He goes into the bedroom and comes back with an empty storage box.

He goes to the kitchen and comes out with a trash bag.

He puts the soccer ball into the empty storage box.

Lights up on Emily, in another place. Baby in a sling.

EMILY: They say you don't remember things like that –

Pain. Crisis. Once it's over. But that's bullshit. You remember. You just don't re-experience. So people say they don't remember because when they think about it, they aren't in the same pain they were in at that moment. But they don't not remember.

I remember.

(Clark begins to dismantle the piles of junk he has guarded for so long.

Trash goes into the trash bag.

Magazines, mail, takeout containers.)

EMILY (Cont.): Clark brought me to the hospital. He didn't want to, I knew that, but he's also not the asshole he makes himself out to be. I knew he wouldn't leave me if Richard wasn't there yet, even though he kept saying it was time to go, he should go, he wasn't leaving, he stayed… he told me to push and didn't look away when everything got - got rough…

I remember.

(The top few layers are gone.

He finds a sock. Jake's sock. He holds it a moment.

He puts that carefully into the box.

Clark finds more papers and junk to put in the trash bag.)

Clark letting me squeeze his hand in a way that couldn't have not hurt

Because it hurt. I hurt. I was tearing apart.

I remember

EMILY (Cont.): and another hand on my arm that was so familiar – a hand that I never thought I'd feel again.

(Clark finds Jake's shirt.

He folds it and carefully puts it in the box)

I looked into his eyes. Into his shit-eating-going-to-need-years-of-braces grin.

(Clark finds a drawing Jake made and puts it in the box.)

He talked me through it.
When the pain hit he helped me ride the wave.
His hair has gotten long, and he's tall, taller than me, I bet. He had some zits on his forehead.
I know –
I know.

But I also know.

That what it felt like was him – in my life again. In my life again.

I remember.

EMILY (Cont.): And then the world changed. Again.

The apartment is becoming a different place than we've seen it be until now.
It is less apartment and more edge of the soccer field, edge of the world.

(Clark picks up the device.

He puts it into the box.

The baby cries. Emily looks at Clark. Clark looks at Emily.)

END OF PLAY

NoPassport Press is an unincorporated theatre alliance and press founded by playwright Caridad Svich. It publishes new plays, translations and essays on theatre and performance. It was founded and has been publishing under the lulu.com imprint since 2003.

CPSIA information can be obtained
at www.ICGtesting.com
Printed in the USA
LVHW101107260123
737853LV00003B/623

9 781458 348548